FRIENDSHIP CURSIVE
HANDWRITING PRACTICE
WORKBOOK

JULIE HARPER

Friendship Cursive Handwriting Practice Workbook

Cover design and illustrations by Melissa Stevens
www.theillustratedauthor.net
Write. Create. Illustrate.

Children's Books > Education & Reference > Words & Language
Children's Books > Education & Reference > Workbooks

ISBN-10: 1503067416
ISBN-13: 978-1503067417

CONTENTS

INTRODUCTION

The goal of this workbook is to inspire anyone's—not just kids, but teens and even adults (since, sadly, cursive handwriting is no longer taught in many schools)—interest in learning and practicing cursive handwriting. Friendship is one theme with which everybody can relate. Applying a theme such as friendship to a workbook helps to make learning fun, whether in the classroom or at home.

Friendship Cursive Handwriting Practice Workbook begins with basic practice of individual letters and gradually builds up to more advanced writing with complete sentences—including a chapter where students must rewrite printed sentences in cursive and a final chapter with writing prompts that encourage cursive writing practice.

Six chapters of this workbook help students develop their cursive writing skills in six steps:

- Part 1 begins with practice tracing and copying letters.
- Part 2 consists of tracing and copying words.
- Part 3 progresses onto tracing and copying phrases.
- Part 4 advances onto short sentences without tracing.
- Part 5 challenges students to rewrite printed text in cursive.
- Part 6 includes writing prompts to encourage cursive practice.

May your students or children (or you!) improve their handwriting skills and enjoy reading and writing these friendship-themed writing exercises.

Uppercase Cursive Alphabet

A B C D E F

G H I J K L

M N O P Q R

S T U V W X

Y Z

Lowercase Cursive Alphabet

a   b   c   d   e   f

g   h   i   j   k   l

m   n   o   p   q   r

s   t   u   v   w   x

y   z

PART 1

Trace and Copy Letters

Instructions: First trace each letter and then copy each letter onto the blank line below. Use the three horizontal lines as a guide for the letter heights.

a a a a a a a

a a a a a a a

C c C c C c C c C

C c C c C c C c C

Call Access Care Ask

  10

O o O o O o O o O

O o O o O o O o O

P p P p P p P p

P p P p P p P p

Pool Open Papa Once

U u U u U u U

U u U u U u U

U u U u U u U

U u U u U u U

Up Would Usual Wow

E e E e E e E e E e E

E e E e E e E e E e E

T t T t T t T t T

T t T t T t T t T

Eat Teeth Each Teach

F f F f F f F f F

F f F f F f F f F

S s S s S s S s S s

S s S s S s S s S s

Safe Feast Seat Fact

M m M m M m

M m M m M m

N n N n N n

N n N n N n

Name Mom Noon Man

B b B b B b B b

B b B b B b B b

D d D d D d D d

D d D d D d D d

Baby Dad Bed Dot

$\mathcal{L}$ $\mathcal{l}$ $\mathcal{L}$ $\mathcal{l}$ $\mathcal{L}$ $\mathcal{l}$ $\mathcal{L}$ $\mathcal{l}$

$\mathcal{L}$ $\mathcal{l}$ $\mathcal{L}$ $\mathcal{l}$ $\mathcal{L}$ $\mathcal{l}$ $\mathcal{L}$ $\mathcal{l}$

$\mathcal{H}$ $\mathcal{h}$ $\mathcal{H}$ $\mathcal{h}$ $\mathcal{H}$ $\mathcal{h}$ $\mathcal{H}$ $\mathcal{h}$

$\mathcal{H}$ $\mathcal{h}$ $\mathcal{H}$ $\mathcal{h}$ $\mathcal{H}$ $\mathcal{h}$ $\mathcal{H}$ $\mathcal{h}$

Heal Let Help Lead

R n R n R n R n R n

R n R n R n R n R n

K k K k K k K k K k

K k K k K k K k K k

Rake Keep Rank Kind

I i I i I i I i I

I i I i I i I i I

J j J j J j J j J

J j J j J j J j J

Idea Join Inside Joy

G g G g G g G

G g G g G g G

Q q Q q Q q Q q

Q q Q q Q q Q q

Good Quiet Goal Quick

$\mathcal{V}$ u $\mathcal{V}$ u $\mathcal{V}$ u $\mathcal{V}$ u

$\mathcal{V}$ u $\mathcal{V}$ u $\mathcal{V}$ u $\mathcal{V}$ u

$\mathcal{X}$ x $\mathcal{X}$ x $\mathcal{X}$ x $\mathcal{X}$ x

$\mathcal{X}$ x $\mathcal{X}$ x $\mathcal{X}$ x $\mathcal{X}$ x

Van X-ray Vote Exist

Y y Y y Y y Y y

Y y Y y Y y Y y

Z z Z z Z z Z z

Z z Z z Z z Z z

Zoo You Zany Breezy

Aa Bb Cc Dd Ee

Ff Gg Hh Ii Jj

Kk Ll Mm Nn Oo

Pp Qq Rr Ss Tt Uu

Vv Ww Xx Yy Zz

Aa Bb Cc Dd Ee

Ff Gg Hh Ii Jj

Kk Ll Mm Nn Oo

Pp Qq Rr Ss Tt Uu

Vv Ww Xx Yy Zz

Aa Bb Cc Dd Ee

Ff Gg Hh Ii Jj

Kk Ll Mm Nn Oo

Pp Qq Rr Ss Tt Uu

Vv Ww Xx Yy Zz

PART 2

Trace and Copy Words

Instructions: First trace each word and then copy each word onto the blank line below. Use the three horizontal lines as a guide for the letter heights.

Amazing Advice Angel

Best Buddies Bond

Caring Close Cheerful

Dependable Delighted

Enjoy Excited Entertain

Fair Friend Faithful

Good Great Glad

Heart Help Honesty

Ideals Impress Include

Joy Joking Justice

Kind Knowing Kinship

Loyal Listen Like

Merry Music Mirth

Nice Note New Neat

Offer Open Opportunity

Peace Patient Promise

Quiet Quality Quickly

Responsible Reassure

Supportive Special

Two Treat Thanks Try

Unique Unity Uplifting

Value Very Virtue

Wise Warm Wish

Xylophone Youthful

Zestful Zeal Zany

Forever

Remarkable

Inseparable

Extraordinary

Nicest and Dearest

  33

Considerate

Wonderful

Treasured

Heartwarming

Kindhearted

  34

Understanding

Compassionate

Appreciative

Togetherness

Unconditional

Supportive

Thoughtful

Meaningful

Affectionate

Comforting

  36

Attentive

Harmonious

Amiable

Inspirational

Cherished

Companionship

Benevolence

Loving

Committed

Trustworthy

  38

Honorable

Sympathetic

Grateful

Reassuring

Smiling

  39

PART 3

Trace and Copy Phrases

Instructions: First trace each phrase and then copy each phrase onto the blank line below.

Shake hands

High-five

Wave goodbye

Pat on the back

Thumbs up

 42

Call me tomorrow.

Talk to you later.

Leave a message.

Have time to talk?

Get my text?

  43

Way to go

That's precious

Thank you

Pretty please

Try it again

Hang out together

Game night

Watch a movie

Meet for lunch

Busy tomorrow?

You sure can

My pleasure

How sweet!

Why not?

What are friends for?

Come back soon.

Don't go far.

Stay calm.

How are you?

Are you having fun?

Best friends forever

Helping hands

Thinking of you

Getting along

Sharing smiles

Offer encouragement

Generous heart

Happy days together

Thankful for you

Lifelong bond

True friends

Give and take

Wonderful memories

Sweet dreams

Forever my friend

  50

Warmth and caring

Sharing secrets

Thoughtful person

Good listener

Undivided attention

Non-judgmental

Reaching out

Caring for you

Taking care

Happy times

  52

Feeling well

Celebrate friendship

Joyous occasions

High spirits

Stuck like glue

Lasting bond

Supporting you

Good friends

Shared understanding

Love and happiness

  54

Sisterhood and brotherhood

Sisters are forever

Brothers are forever

Lucky to know you

One-of-a-kind friend

Watching out for you

Sharing emotions

Helping to heal wounds

Forever in my heart

Love, laughter, friends

  56

You make me smile.

You are my sunshine.

We give each other strength.

I will take care of you.

You understand me.

Enjoy the good times.

Friends bring smiles.

You're my friend forever.

Open your heart.

You will never be alone.

Together it can be done.

The feeling is mutual.

Trust your friends.

I identify with you.

I'm never alone.

We cry together.

We enjoy laughter.

You offer support.

You understand me.

You always inspire me.

Friends give hope.

Friends show they care.

Friends are always sincere.

True friends are priceless.

Together we stand.

Laugh out loud together.

Emit warm feelings.

Friends aren't judgmental.

True friendship never fades.

You're always by my side.

  62

Let's sing and dance.

You give me hope.

You're my best buddy.

Thanks for being you.

You make me smile.

You are my best friend.

You know my secrets.

You keep my secrets.

We can trust each other.

Life is beautiful.

  64

You're so good to me.

You are one in a million.

You're the greatest.

You mean the world to me.

I'm fortunate to know you.

Our friendship is golden.

I talk. You listen intently.

You give me direction.

You understand me.

You know when to talk.

  66

Make someone smile.

Give your heart.

Take time to be happy.

Let love blossom.

Friends bring happiness.

PART 4

Copy Sentences without Tracing

Instructions: Copy the sentences onto the blank lines below. This chapter is not designed for tracing.

The A, B, C's of friendship...

My best friend...

Appreciates me...

Brings out the best in me...

Cares how I feel...

Delivers on promises...

Enjoys our time together...

Forgives and forgets...

Gives good advice...

Has a huge heart...

Isn't selfish...

Jokes at the right time...

Keeps me smiling...

Laughs with me...

Means the world to me...

Never criticizes me...

Only wants the best for me...

Patiently waits for me...

Quickly comes to my rescue...

Roots for me...

Stands up for me...

Together we stand...

Understands me...

Values our friendship...

Will always be here for me...

X-tra special to me...

Yours truly,

3-best friend ever!

You are the best.

The A to Z's of friendship.

  75

You are awesome just

the way you are.

Don't ever change.

Thanks for being you.

We understand each other.

True friends last forever.

We are side-by-side during

the good and bad days.

It's great being your friend.

Thanks for being my friend.

You taught me to love

myself. You gave me the

confidence to believe in

myself. You help me

fulfill my dreams. Thanks.

You bring out the best in

me. I hope I do the same

for you. You are the best

thing in my life.

Very best friends forever.

You hold me up, and

keep me from falling.

You give me the strength

to go forward when the

times are tough.

  80

Best friends are good for

each other. Give thanks.

We take time out for each

other, and enjoy every

moment together.

You asked what I wanted

for my birthday.

I answered, "I have

everything I need because

I have your friendship."

Have I ever told you how

much you mean to me?

You are the most important

person in the world.

You mean the world to me.

Take pleasure in the little

things in life.

Enjoy them with your

loved ones.

Enjoy life with your friends.

The best memories are the

ones made with my friends.

The joy of true friendship

is wonderful.

Friends are priceless.

You've seen my good,

bad, and ugly, but you

still love me.

Thanking you for being my

best friend through it all.

You are always with me.

Distance can't keep us

apart. You are always close

to my heart no matter

how far apart we are.

It's so wonderful knowing

that I can trust you with

my innermost secrets.

Thank you for never

criticizing or judging me.

A friend accepts your past,

is there for you today,

and encourages your

plans and dreams for

the future.

I ask myself, "What did

I do to deserve you?"

I'm so lucky to have you

for my best friend.

You're a dream come true!

I will always be by your

side during good times

and not so good times

no matter what happens.

It's you and I together.

I wish I could put into

words how much you

mean to me.

I value your friendship

more than words can say.

We may not see each other,

or talk to one another

every day, but you are

always in my thoughts.

You mean so much to me.

I can't thank you enough

for being here whenever

I need a helping hand,

or a hug, or someone to

laugh and talk to.

  94

I am the happiest person

when I am with you.

I am blessed to have

you for my best friend.

You are so special to me.

A friend knows how to

speak frankly without

hurting your feelings...

and how to make

you feel good about yourself.

  96

Every day, you put a little

sunshine into my life.

You are my sunshine.

The sun shines on me

even on cloudy days.

My true friends let me

be myself. They accept

me for who I am. They

don't try to change me. I

can be myself around them.

A friend helps lead you

down the right path.

A friend is always there

to offer support without

being critical.

I am thankful for the

positive friendships that

have enriched my life.

I am blessed to have

such wonderful friends.

  100

Take time to thank your

friends for bringing you

so much joy and happiness.

Let them know how

important they are to you.

PART 5

Rewrite Printed Sentences in Cursive

Instructions: Rewrite each printed sentence in cursive handwriting onto the blank lines below. Refer to pages vi-vii as needed. Check your answers at the end of the book.

The beauty of a friend

is the best gift of all.

You've touched my heart.

Our friendship is priceless.

Thank you for being you.

Let's enjoy a wonderful

day together.

Kick back and relax.

Just take pleasure in

being together.

Our circle of friendship

grows and grows.

We stick together.

We will always take care

of each other.

Take time to appreciate

your friends.

Let them know how much

they mean to you.

Give thanks.

My friend, the good

listener. You are honest

and true. You always

offer meaningful and

well-intentioned advice.

We are inseparable.

We may not be physically

together, but our hearts

are always tied together.

My heart loves you.

  109

We have love and trust

for each other.

We are loyal to one another.

You are my loyal friend.

Thank you for your honesty.

You love my strengths,

and strengthen my

weaknesses.

I thank you for loving

me the way I am.

I never have a lonely

day because you are always

with me in my heart.

I opened my heart to you.

You opened your arms to me.

Dreaming of you.

You help make all of

my dreams come true.

May all of your dreams

come true.

You enrich my life.

My life is fuller because

of you.

My life has been enhanced

because of you.

You help me visualize

my dreams, and help

me make them come true.

You give me hope when

I am feeling down.

We can do it together.

You give me the confidence

to take on new ventures.

I will always support

you and your dreams.

Compassionate, kind,

considerate, and caring

are just a few words that

describe my best friend.

You are my best friend.

My friend is the one I

can share my innermost

secrets with.

...who will not judge me.

...who is always here for me.

I will always hold you

close to my heart.

I treasure our memories.

I know we will keep

making new memories.

I can be myself when

I'm with my friends.

My friends accept me

for who I am. I accept

them for who they are.

I'm surrounded by love

thanks to my friends.

I will always treasure

my true friends.

Best friends forever!

Be grateful for your friends.

I can't thank you enough

for being here whenever

I need a helping hand,

or someone to talk to.

Treat your friends well.

I will always treasure

my very dear friends.

We are best friends forever.

Happiness grows.

Make new friends.

Welcome them to your

circle of friends.

Let your friendships

grow stronger each day.

My 'bestie' knows how I

feel by just looking at me.

I don't have to utter a

word. My 'bestie' is always

here to offer encouragement.

I think my 'bestie' can

read my mind.

Sometimes I think my

'bestie' understands me

better than I do myself.

You help me make my

dreams come true.

You believed in me when

others thought I was crazy.

Thanks for the support!

My best friend knows

how to make me smile

no matter what happens.

My friend can always turn

a frown into a smile.

  128

We enjoy each other's

company regardless of where

we are, or what we're doing.

Sometimes we just spend

quiet time together.

You are my everything.

You bring me happiness.

You give me comfort

when I need it.

You mean the world to me.

I'm here...

When you need a hug.

When you need to talk.

When you need me to

be there for you.

Your friendship is a very

precious gift to me.

I will always treasure

our wonderful friendship.

You are my best friend.

You always find a way

to put a smile on my face.

You wipe away my tears.

You bring so much

happiness into my life.

PART 6

Cursive Writing Prompts

Instructions: These writing prompts are designed to offer practice composing and writing sentences in cursive handwriting. Refer to pages vi-vii as needed.

Prompt 1. Describe one of your friends.

Prompt 2. Describe something fun that you do with friends.

Prompt 3. Describe where you and your friends get together.

Prompt 4. What's a big plan that you and a friend have?

Prompt 5. What do friends do that make you feel better?

Prompt 6. When and how did you meet one of your friends?

Prompt 7. Remember one of the first friends you ever made.

Prompt 8. What kinds of things do you look for in a friend?

Prompt 9. Describe a funny thing that involved friends.

Prompt 10. Describe a time when your friends surprised you.

Prompt 11. Make up a short story involving friends.

Continue your short story on this page.

Prompt 12. Write a poem about friendship.

Prompt 13. Pick a friend. What do you like about this friend?

Prompt 14. Make up a story about meeting a new friend.

Continue your story on this page.

Prompt 15. Describe something you did with a friend recently.

Prompt 16. What are the best things about friendship?

Prompt 17. Describe how you celebrate with your friends.

Continue your story on this page.

Prompt 18. Remember a wonderful time you had with friends.

Continue your story on this page.

Prompt 19. Make up a story that shows the value of friendship.

Continue your story on this page.

Prompt 20. Write a story about making a new friend.

Continue your story on this page.

Prompt 21. Imagine doing something exciting with a friend.

Continue your story on this page.

Prompt 22. Write a story about unlikely friends.

Continue your story on this page.

Prompt 23. What do you plan to do with a friend soon?

Continue your story on this page.

THANK YOU!

We sincerely thank you for reading Julie Harper's book, *Friendship Cursive Handwriting Practice Workbook.*

Our team worked very hard on this book: Julie wrote the exercises, an editor proofread them, a typographer formatted the interior, Melissa Stevens designed the cover and illustrated the book, and feedback from people like you helped develop the exercises into their current shape.

Everyone on this team would be very appreciative if you would please share your feedback on this book in a review at Amazon, Goodreads, a blog (if you have one), or anywhere else you would feel comfortable expressing feedback.

We hope that your children or students (or you!) enjoyed this book. Thank you very much for using it. ☺

ANSWERS TO PART 5

Page 104

The beauty of a friend
is the best gift of all.
You've touched my heart.
Our friendship is priceless.
Thank you for being you.

Page 105

Let's enjoy a wonderful
day together.
Kick back and relax.
Just take pleasure in
being together.

Page 106

Our circle of friendship
grows and grows.
We stick together.
We will always take care
of each other.

Page 107

Take time to appreciate
your friends.
Let them know how much
they mean to you.
Give thanks.

Page 108

My friend, the good
listener. You are honest
and true. You always
offer meaningful and
well-intentioned advice.

Page 109

We are inseparable.
We may not be physically
together, but our hearts
are always tied together.
My heart loves you.

Page 110

We have love and trust
for each other.
We are loyal to one another.
You are my loyal friend.
Thank you for your honesty.

Page 111

You love my strengths,
and strengthen my
weaknesses.
I thank you for loving
me the way I am.

Page 112

I never have a lonely
day because you are always
with me in my heart.
I opened my heart to you.
You opened your arms to me.

Page 113

Dreaming of you.
You help make all of
my dreams come true.
May all of your dreams
come true.

Page 114

You enrich my life.
My life is fuller because
of you.
My life has been enhanced
because of you.

Page 115

You help me visualize
my dreams, and help
me make them come true.
You give me hope when
I am feeling down.

Page 116

We can do it together.
You give me the confidence
to take on new ventures.
I will always support
you and your dreams.

Page 117

Compassionate, kind,
considerate, and caring
are just a few words that
describe my best friend.
You are my best friend.

Page 118

My friend is the one I
can share my innermost
secrets with.
...who will not judge me.
...who is always here for me.

Page 119

I will always hold you
close to my heart.
I treasure our memories.
I know we will keep
making new memories.

Page 120

I can be myself when
I'm with my friends.
My friends accept me
for who I am. I accept
them for who they are.

Page 121

I'm surrounded by love
thanks to my friends.
I will always treasure
my true friends.
Best friends forever!

Page 122

Be grateful for your friends.
I can't thank you enough
for being here whenever
I need a helping hand,
or someone to talk to.

Page 123

Treat your friends well.
I will always treasure
my very dear friends.
We are best friends forever.
Happiness grows.

Page 124

Make new friends.
Welcome them to your
circle of friends.
Let your friendships
grow stronger each day.

Page 125

My 'bestie' knows how I
feel by just looking at me.
I don't have to utter a
word. My 'bestie' is always
here to offer encouragement.

Page 126

I think my 'bestie' can
read my mind.
Sometimes I think my
'bestie' understands me
better than I do myself.

Page 127

You help me make my
dreams come true.
You believed in me when
others thought I was crazy.
Thanks for the support!

Page 128

My best friend knows
how to make me smile
no matter what happens.
My friend can always turn
a frown into a smile.

Page 129

We enjoy each other's
company regardless of where
we are, or what we're doing.
Sometimes we just spend
quiet time together.

Page 130

You are my everything.
You bring me happiness.
You give me comfort
when I need it.
You mean the world to me.

Page 131

I'm here...
When you need a hug.
When you need to talk.
When you need me to
be there for you.

Page 132

Your friendship is a very
precious gift to me.
I will always treasure
our wonderful friendship.
You are my best friend.

Page 133

You always find a way
to put a smile on my face.
You wipe away my tears.
You bring so much
happiness into my life.

JULIE HARPER BOOKS

wackysentences.com

amazon.com/author/julieharper

Printing Practice:

Printing Practice Handwriting Workbook for Girls.

Printing Practice Handwriting Workbook for Boys.

Tongue Twisters Printing Practice Writing Workbook.

Print Uppercase and Lowercase Letters, Words, and Silly Phrases:

Kindergarten and First Grade Writing Practice Workbook (Reproducible).

Print Wacky Sentences: First and Second Grade Writing Practice

Workbook (Reproducible).

Cursive Handwriting:

Letters, Words, and Silly Phrases Handwriting Workbook (Reproducible):

Practice Writing in Cursive (Second and Third Grade).

Wacky Sentences Handwriting Workbook (Reproducible):

Practice Writing in Cursive (Third and Fourth Grade).

Cursive Handwriting Workbook for Girls.

Cursive Handwriting Practice Workbook for Teens.

Spooky Cursive Handwriting Practice Workbook.

Cursive Handwriting Practice Workbook for Boys.

Reading & Writing:

Reading Comprehension for Girls.

Read Wacky Sentences Basic Reading Comprehension Workbook.

Wacky Creative Writing Assignments Workbook.

Reading Comprehension for Girls

Cursive Handwriting Practice Workbook for Teens

35892292R00099

Made in the USA
Middletown, DE
18 October 2016